Original title:
Secrets in the Spruce

Copyright © 2025 Creative Arts Management OÜ
All rights reserved.

Author: Franklin Stone
ISBN HARDBACK: 978-1-80567-366-8
ISBN PAPERBACK: 978-1-80567-665-2

Beneath the Bark, a World Unknown

In the realm where critters dwell,
Tiny gnomes ring a tiny bell.
Squirrels plot and dance around,
While the trees just stand their ground.

Mice wear hats that are too big,
Waltzing slow, a clumsy jig.
Underneath the bark they scheme,
Making plans like a wild dream.

Intrigues of the Rooted Beings

The roots gossip without a care,
While the thorns are plotting flair.
Creepy crawlies roll their eyes,
At the tall tales of the skies.

A family of ants holds court,
Debating if they need a fort.
With leaves as parchment, they shall write,
A secret guide to win the plight.

The Soft Spelling of Shade

In the cool where shadows flit,
A raccoon's hat fits just a bit.
Silly whispers breeze through leaves,
As the barky tree just heaves.

Chasing squirrels, a playful game,
While ants carry snack-sized fame.
Fungi giggle without a sound,
Rooting for a party found.

Whispers of the Woodland Heart

A toad croaks out the latest news,
While hedgehogs wear their finest shoes.
Beneath a leaf a party's set,
And all the critters can't forget.

The owl just hoots a silly tune,
While fireflies dance with the moon.
In the brush, they share a cheer,
For fun is found where friends are near.

The Mysteries Woven in Branches

In the forest, whispers hum,
Squirrels plot with each other, oh what fun!
A raccoon's prank, a secret stash,
Tales of acorns and the occasional splash.

Beneath the bark, a riddle lies,
A woodpecker's laugh, much to our surprise.
He knocks and taps with such delight,
While shy rabbits giggle out of sight.

The old owl giggles from her tree,
Who knew the woods could be so spry and free?
With tangled vines and roots up high,
They share their secrets, oh my, oh my!

In every shadow, a whisper sings,
The great pine shakes with wild wings.
Nature's joke, a playful jest,
In the woods, we are truly blessed!

Echoing Lullabies in the Glade

In the glade where shadows play,
A chorus of critters finds their way.
Frogs compose a croaky tune,
While fireflies dance beneath the moon.

Breezes carry giggles far and wide,
As chipmunks scurry, trying to hide.
They trip and tumble in foolish fun,
Who knew forest antics could weigh a ton?

The grass tickles as we all lay low,
Jaw-dropping tales of the mighty crow.
With each rustle, laughter rings,
In the night, the forest sings.

From under the leaves, a secret spills,
A tale of chaos and playful thrills.
As stars twinkle, we can't resist,
The funny antics in this woodland twist!

The Spirit of the Elder Pines

Among the pines, old jokes resound,
Where wise winds play and dance around.
A squirrel spins tales, truly absurd,
Of forgotten nuts and a snoozy bird.

Branches gossip in fluttering leaves,
While the cheeky deer sneak through the eaves.
They snicker softly at what they see,
A playful spirit in every tree.

Down by the roots, a mystery stirs,
With giggles shared by the little furs.
Each branch holds tales of trouble and glee,
In this piney realm, oh can't you see?

As sunlight spills through needles high,
The trees chuckle low, oh my, oh my!
In this sanctuary where secrets bloom,
Joyful laughter fills every room!

The Keeper of Hidden Roots

In the forest where whispers dance,
A squirrel plots its sneaky chance.
With acorns buried, oh what fun,
Hiding treasures from everyone.

The trunks are full of giggles low,
As critters trade their tales, you know.
A rabbit's joke, a mole's surprise,
In the wood, laughter subtly lies.

Each rustle holds a playful scheme,
Like a woodland's most mischievous dream.
The keeper chuckles, what a sight,
As woodland games go into the night.

Lost Words in the Wilderness

Words float like feathers on the breeze,
Caught in the branches with such ease.
A robin chirps a rhyming spree,
While fawns giggle beneath the trees.

A lost phrase here, a quip misplaced,
Each silence filled with words embraced.
Porcupines ponder with raised quills,
As everyone snickers, oh what thrills!

Bees buzz in verses, sweet as pie,
While wise old owls croon from the sky.
In this wild world, we lose our place,
Yet find pure joy in nature's grace.

Nature's Quiet Confidant

Among soft leaves and shadows long,
A wise old tree hums a secret song.
Mice scurry by with tiny thrills,
While the beetle taps out quirky drills.

Whispered laughter fills the air,
In every branch, a friendly stare.
A chipmunk winks, a playful tease,
As rustling jokes bring hearts to ease.

The trunk's a diary, bark-lined with cheer,
Each scar a tale of the year.
In this cozy nook, so sublime,
Nature's jesters bide their time.

The Enchanted Green Cathedral

In a hall where branches intertwine,
Mossy pews echo the divine.
Frogs in robes croak a funny rhyme,
As the sunbeams dance in perfect time.

The choir sings with chirps so bright,
While beetles twirl in pure delight.
Squirrels take their front row seat,
For the grand show, oh what a treat!

Candles flicker—fireflies flash,
A raccoon chef prepares a splash.
In this playful, leafy space,
Nature's antics leave a trace.

Beneath the Veil of the Foliage

In the thicket where whispers play,
Squirrels gossip about their day.
A raccoon dons a mask so sly,
Poking fun at passersby.

The chickadees with a cheerful peep,
Share their tales, a giggle heap.
Beneath the branches' green embrace,
Nature's clown in leafy space.

A fox with swagger, struts along,
While frogs join in with a ribbit song.
Every rustle hides a tale,
In foliage where humor prevails.

Amidst the trees where laughter grows,
The antics of owls nobody knows.
A forest filled with jests galore,
Celebrate life outside the door.

The Undergrowth's Secret Song

In the shadowed depths, a tune does rise,
Worms wiggling dance with glittery eyes.
A beetle hums a off-key beat,
While crickets tap their tiny feet.

Bouncing bunnies swap silly looks,
As chipmunks read their own comic books.
Every leaf holds a playful tone,
As nature cracks jokes of its own.

The roots entwine in a quirky knot,
Telling tales of the things they've got.
Beneath the canopy, the chuckles flow,
In a symphony only they know.

A caterpillar spins in delight,
Spinning stories until the night.
Within the hush, a funny spark,
Echoes the woodland's joyful lark.

A Saga of the Silent Firs

The fir-studded crowns watch over all,
As a porcupine takes a tumble and falls.
With needles sharp and a quill like flair,
He shakes it off, unaware of the stare.

Among the trunks, a party's planned,
With acorns serving as snacks so grand.
A party hat made of mossy green,
Dancing with glee, quite the funny scene.

The owls hoot in a wise old jest,
While mice perform their silly best.
Under the stars, they gather near,
Sharing laughs in woodland cheer.

In the heart of the forest, joy has sprouted,
Where giggles echo and fears are scouted.
Each tree a witness, each root a friend,
To laughter that will never end.

Tales Weaving Through the Woodlands

Beneath the canopy where stories dwell,
A lizard slips on a leaf—oh, what the hell!
The mushrooms giggle in hues of glee,
As a jumping jack leaps, wild and free.

The shadows stretch with a playful pause,
While woodland critters take a cause.
A sparrow fluffs her feathers bright,
Declaring the trees are quite the sight!

Mice in a line, they scurry about,
Playing tag - their favorite route.
The laughter flows through trunks and fronds,
As nature's sense of humor responds.

In the glade, tales twist and twine,
From ancient bark to fresh pine vine.
Every twig and leaf takes part,
In the forest's funny, joyful heart.

Tales from the Twisted Boughs

In the twisted boughs, the squirrels play,
They plot and scheme the night away.
A nutty heist, they think they're sly,
'Till one drops low and waves goodbye.

A woodpecker thinks he's quite the star,
He drums on trees, a wannabe czar.
But the echoes laugh, a jest so keen,
The rest just chirp, "He'll never be seen."

The rabbits gossip, they can't be shy,
About a fox who's lost his tie.
Dressed in leaves, he tried to blend,
But his bushy tail was quite the trend!

And when the moon shines all aglow,
The pinecones chuckle, putting on a show.
With ticklish winds and playful gales,
They dance in circles, telling their tales.

Shadows Among the Needles

In shadows deep where whispers creep,
A raccoon tells a tale so cheap.
"I've seen the owl wear mismatched socks,
And dance with mice around the rocks!"

A hedgehog scowls with spiky pride,
"Those owls can't hide; I'm the night's guide!
They think they're cool with their big wise eyes,
But I saw one trip, oh, what a surprise!"

The thickets rustle with laughter loud,
As a deer trips over, all too proud.
She spins and prances with grace anew,
Till the fawns giggle, saying, "Who knew?"

When twilight falls, and fears look grim,
The shadows share a laugh on a whim.
For nature's jest is quite absurd,
A forest life with humor stirred.

Soft Confessions of the Forest

In the forest's heart, a snail did vow,
"I'm the quickest, just watch me now!"
But when a fly zipped by with cheer,
The snail just sighed—"Oh dear, oh dear!"

A porcupine sings a love song bold,
But his quills get stuck, and now he's told.
"Your serenade's the prickle of fate,
Please stick to whispers, don't tempt your state!"

The frogs croak tales of daring leaps,
While the shy bats giggle, counting sheep.
"A splash! A jump! What grace! What flair!
Now just look at what's in my hair!"

As night descends, with jokes divine,
The trees conspire—this fun's all mine!
With giggles shared beneath the moon,
The forest sings a merry tune.

Murmurs in the Moss

Mossy patches whisper and sigh,
"Did you hear? That owl can't fly!"
A crow cackles, wings spread wide,
"I've seen him try—what a strange ride!"

A ladybug boasts of her swift grand tour,
"I'm off to the party—oh, I'm so mature!"
But she gets distracted, in the dew she sits,
While the ants parade, saying, "Look at her hits!"

The fox struts by, a tail in the air,
"I'm the slyest here, beyond compare!"
But tripping on roots, he stumbles with flair,
"Perhaps another path, if I dare!"

As ferns swish and twirl in jest,
The woods come alive, a vibrant fest.
So if you hear a chuckle or two,
Just smile and nod—the forest is true!

Secrets of the Sylvan Heart

In a forest where the laughter roams,
Squirrels plot in leafy homes.
They gossip with the chirping birds,
Whispering tales without a word.

A raccoon wears a clever hat,
As he tiptoes near a sleeping cat.
The trees hold back their painted grins,
While the mischief truly begins.

Beneath the branches, shadows dance,
While bunnies play their silly prance.
Frogs croak jokes by the lily brook,
In their world, they'd write a book!

Each rustle hides a giggle fit,
In a realm where creatures commit.
Nature holds its playful throne,
With laughter echoing in each stone.

Hidden Passages of the Evergreens

Amongst the pines where giggles hide,
A fox prepares a grand surprise.
With acorns stacked in great array,
He throws a nutty masquerade!

The owls wear spectacles, very wise,
While raccoons schmooze with bright green ties.
"Who wore it best?" they slyly shout,
As woodland fashion rings about.

A bear in slippers, quite a sight,
Dances barefoot in the light.
Trees chuckle softly, roots entwined,
While all of nature's quirks unwind.

Squirrels juggling nuts on stage,
And woodland creatures setting the age.
Here in the thicket, jesters thrive,
In these places, laughter's alive!

The Silent Symphonies of the Woods

Beneath the bows, a string of glee,
Where beetles strum and ants agree.
The sunbeam plays the flute so bright,
And whispers join the woodpeckers' flight.

A hedgehog hums a little tune,
As leaves all dance and sway by noon.
The grasshoppers join, legs in sync,
Creating rhythms, all in pink!

With mushrooms as their clever stage,
The critters act without a rage.
A squirrel stars in comic role,
In leafy laughter, they all stroll.

Echoes of joy in splintered barks,
And flashes of whimsy in the parks.
In wooded halls, the silliness sings,
In harmonious love, every crevice brings.

Cloaked in Green: A Woodland Story

Amidst the ferns, a tale unfolds,
Of mushrooms dancing in greens and golds.
The crickets chirp a cheerful beat,
Their tiny legs tapping in the heat.

A turtle tells of treasure lost,
A map that drew the creatures tossed.
They gathered at dawn with plans so grand,
To find the loot, all hand in hand.

The owls hoot loudly, passing notes,
While gathering clouds shape whimsical boats.
A raccoon's theatrics grab the day,
For laughter keeps the gloom at bay.

Beneath twigged roofs, the whispers plan,
With each twist and turn, a giggling clan.
Nature gleefully sways, note for note,
In cloaks of green, where heartbeats float.

Unraveled Threads of Nature's Veil

In the woods where whispers play,
A squirrel wears a hat today.
He grins and twirls, oh what a sight,
Chasing shadows, a comical flight.

The branches giggle, they sway and tease,
While ants march in a line to please.
A rabbit hops, with flair so grand,
Hiding treasures in the sand.

The mushrooms dance, a quirky crew,
Each with a tale that's funny and true.
Laughter echoes through the green,
In this patch where joy is seen.

Nature pranks, a merry spree,
With every rustle, there's jubilee.
So come along and join the cheer,
In this forest, let fun appear.

Twilight's Secrets in the Treetops

As dusk descends, the owls convene,
A council of wise, with jokes unseen.
They hoot about the tales they've heard,
Of mischievous gnomes and a flying bird.

With twinkling stars and a wink of light,
A raccoon juggles berries at night.
The trees all chuckle in leafy glee,
At wonderment only they can see.

The breeze carries secrets, or so it claims,
Like frogs in hats playing silly games.
Each leaf a partner in a dance so spry,
With every gust, a joyful sigh.

In this twilight, fun takes flight,
With creatures that sparkle, oh what a sight!
So tiptoe softly beneath the glow,
And find the mirth in nature's show.

The Enchantment of Forgotten Paths

On a trail where mischief roams,
A plump little hedgehog calls it home.
With giggles trapped in his quilly spikes,
He tells tall tales of wily hikes.

Under the moss, a snail does race,
Wearing a shell with a smiling face.
They've lost their way, but with a cheer,
They'll find their path, never fear!

In cobwebs spun from laughter's thread,
A spider spins tales, as sweet as bread.
Her web's a stage for a comedy show,
With beetles and bugs in attendance, oh!

With each twist and turn in the fading light,
Silly antics abound, what a delight!
So follow the laughter, let worries cease,
In this enchanting place, find your peace.

Echoes of the Ancient Pines

Amidst the pines, where shadows scheme,
A party happens, like in a dream.
The woodpecker drums a silly beat,
While raccoons dance on little feet.

The branches bend, a secret crew,
Whispering tricks that they will brew.
A fox in a cape, a delightful prank,
He leaps and twirls, then heads to the bank.

The pine needles chuckle, tickling the air,
With whispers of fun, they invite, beware!
The eldest oak shares tales of yore,
Of rabbit races and squirrel lore.

As dusk approaches and stars ignite,
The forest sparkles with sheer delight.
So when you wander, keep your eyes wide,
For laughter and joy in the woods abide.

Mystic Pathways Through the Pines

In the woods where whispers play,
A squirrel's chatter leads the way.
With acorn hats and tricks they share,
The trees, they giggle; they can't help but stare.

A rabbit's dance, oh what a sight,
Doing the tango under moonlight.
The pinecones chuckle as they drop,
Join the party, never stop!

Fairies wink from leafy bower,
While gnomes sip dew at the witching hour.
Each shadow bears a tale untold,
Of mossy pranks and laughter bold.

So skip along the winding trail,
With friends abound, you cannot fail.
A world of whims beneath the bough,
Come laugh with nature—join us now!

Nature's Cradle of Quietude

Cradled soft in leafy arms,
A turtle hums its own sweet charms.
With each slow step, the world wakes up,
While busy birds fly past to sup.

A raccoon plays peekaboo with the dew,
As shadows dance and stars come through.
The owls roll eyes, as if to tease,
Claiming wisdom among the breeze.

Flowers gossip in colors bright,
Tickling bees with pure delight.
Behind each trunk, a giggle sneaks,
Nature's humor, oh so unique!

In whispers soft, the forest chuckles,
Tales of the woods, their joyful ruckles.
With every rustle, a giggle grows,
In this cradle where laughter flows!

Intricate Patterns of the Pinewood

In the convoluted lines of bark,
A woodpecker makes its mark.
Tapping tunes to share the news,
While squirrels scurry, don their shoes.

The twilight casts a puzzling shade,
As critters glide through leaf parade.
A hedgehog spun in playful spins,
While pine needles join in grins.

Fancy fungi wear hats too bright,
Giggling mushrooms greet the night.
Elves in the shadows play their tricks,
With nature's jesters, time ticks.

So walk the paths where laughter's spun,
Among the trees, the wild and fun.
Each twist and turn a playground shown,
In this pinewood, we feel at home!

The Unraveling of the Forest's Folklore

Under the boughs where legends weave,
The wind tells tales for those who believe.
A fox in spectacles reads the scrolls,
While whispers bounce around like moles.

The owl hoots a riddle, quite absurd,
As rabbits laugh, their giggles heard.
Each bush seems to join the jest,
In this forest, it's a wild quest!

Pine cones gossip like they're alive,
Sharing secrets with bees that thrive.
Hidden paths where mischief brews,
Nature's chaos inspires the muse.

So venture forth into the glade,
Where stories blossom, never fade.
With every step, a chuckle's born,
In the roots of laughter, we are sworn!

The Language of Leaves and Shadows

In the trees, whispers rise,
Like giggles caught by surprise.
Branches dance with a cheeky sway,
Leaves gossip in their leafy play.

Squirrels plot with acorn schemes,
Underneath the sun's warm beams.
Toadstools laugh at passing shoes,
While shadows dance, sharing clues.

Beneath the bark, a secret smile,
Woodpecker jokes echo a mile.
Laughter floats on gentle breeze,
A forest full of sneaky tease.

In this grove of playful cheer,
Nature's giggle ear to ear.
Is that a rustle or a jest?
Amongst the trees, we jest the best!

The Cryptic Conversations of Nature

Ferns are whispering all around,
Mossy jokes from the damp ground.
Raccoons chuckle, pulling pranks,
While shadows share their merry thanks.

The owls hoot in wise replies,
Telling tales of lush supplies.
Breezes carry laughter's tune,
Under the watchful eye of the moon.

High above, the chatter flows,
As ants march on in tidy rows.
Frogs croak puns in puddle pools,
While rabbits share their funny rules.

Each twig holds a tale of mirth,
A comedy show beneath the earth.
Nature's jesters, bold and bright,
Keep the forest buzzing with delight!

Preserve of the Whispering Pines

The pines are shaking with delight,
Hiding jokes from first to night.
Breezy banter in the air,
Laughing leaves without a care.

Chipmunks snicker in a tree,
Peeking out, so playfully.
Their wrinkled noses wrinkle more,
As they plot mischief galore.

Bark done up like a grin,
Mischief brewing deep within.
As branches sway, a chuckle spreads,
Creating giggles in cozy beds.

Far above, a feathered jest,
A chorus of chuckles at its best.
In this grove of laughter's kin,
With a wink, let the fun begin!

The Forest's Covert Chronicles

In the woods, where shadows wink,
Mischievous thoughts begin to blink.
Twigs snap with a playful tone,
As if the trees are not alone.

Hedgehogs huddle, sharing tales,
Of tiny pranks and silly fails.
A chipmunk's twist on a simple plan,
Gathering giggles across the span.

The branches creak a merry tune,
Under the sway of a silly moon.
Leaves rustle as they laugh and skate,
Mixing puns with fun sedate.

A playful breeze joins in the fun,
Tickles the grass under the sun.
Each root and rock, a giggling friend,
In this wood, the laughter will never end!

Reveries of the Great Canopy

In the branches, squirrels play,
They hide their treasures, come what may.
A nut or two, perhaps a shoe,
What else they'll find, no one has a clue.

The birds exchange their gossip loud,
While chatting with the passing cloud.
A worm's got tales, a frog can leap,
In this great forest, laughter's deep.

The leaves conspire, they cluck and clamor,
Tickling each twig, with a soft glamour.
A raccoon snores, a deer winks bright,
Oh, what a sight under moonlit night!

So if you wander, be prepared,
To take part in the folly shared.
For under this green, a grand parade,
Of giggles and tricks, simply handmade.

An Overture of Silent Whispers

In shadows, critters dance and prance,
Inviting you to join their chance.
A tumble here, a slide on bark,
Every sound, a joyful lark.

The shadows play a game of hide,
While pinecones tumble, side to side.
A chattering crowd of furry friends,
With punchlines waiting, laughter bends.

The moss blooms plush, a velvet throne,
Whiskered owls in a hushed tone.
A party of crickets starts to sing,
Melodies sweet, on fragile wing.

So join the fun beneath the trees,
Where giggles float upon the breeze.
A world where whispers bounce and twirl,
A joyous tapestry, unfurled!

Whispers Beneath the Canopy

Beneath the leaves, a mystery brews,
As chipmunks gather, sharing news.
With tiny paws, they plot tall tales,
Of missing cheese and lost email trails.

The fungi laugh in shadowed glades,
While sneaky shadows play charades.
A dance of ants, in a line so neat,
Boy, can they move those little feet!

The breeze joins in, a friendly tease,
Tugging at branches with gentle ease.
A skip, a hop, a raucous cheer,
Echoes of fun, for all to hear.

So if you linger, don't be shy,
Join in the jest, don't let it fly.
For in this realm of giggles and fuss,
The laughter spreads, infectious for us!

The Hidden Echoes of Evergreen

In tangled roots, a story spins,
Of hedgehogs dancing, grins on skins.
A beetle shares his world-renowned,
The biggest berry he ever found!

The squirrels swoosh with acrobatic flair,
Creating giggles, light as air.
With every leap, tales tumble down,
Crafting laughter, a leafy crown.

The bushes rustle, a mystery grows,
With conversations only nature knows.
A gentle breeze carries sweet delight,
Where every whisper ignites the night.

So come and frolic, don't be late,
In this realm of whimsy, celebrate.
With every echo that brightly sings,
You might just find joy that nature brings.

The Breath of the Whispering Pines

In the woods where shadows play,
Trees gossip in a breezy way.
A squirrel giggles, hangs a sign,
"Nut thieves beware, this place is mine!"

Branches dance with a silly sway,
Barking dogs join the fray.
A raccoon tips his hat with pride,
As deer roll eyes, too dignified.

Mice in tuxedos, they arrange,
A party wild, it feels so strange.
With acorn hats and twiggy bows,
They twirl beneath the sprouting crows.

So listen close, hear the cheer,
In these trees, humor's near.
The breath of pines holds laughter bright,
In their whispers, joy takes flight.

Intrigues of the Evergreen Haven

Underneath the green-clad guise,
Lies a plot that will surprise.
A beetle dressed in a top hat winks,
As ladybugs share juicy links.

Chipmunks meet to trade some cheese,
Laughing under frosty leaves.
A hedgehog's wearing shoes too tight,
Stumbles, causing quite a sight!

A tale spins among the fronds,
Of parties held beyond the beyonds.
With pine cone crowns, they plan a spree,
Underneath the tallest tree.

With laughter tickling the cool air,
They dance and prance without a care.
In this haven, joy unfolds,
As evergreen intrigues are retold.

Hidden Realms Beneath the Cones

Beneath the canopy so grand,
A treasure trove, not just for hand.
With socks and spoons in playful stash,
A raccoon bids his friends to dash.

Amidst the roots, old tales emerge,
Of mischief that they love to purge.
A gopher's got a gig, so sly,
With a wink and a nod, oh my, oh my!

The pine cones roll with laughter loud,
While a weasel tackles a huge crowd.
A secret realm of tricks and glee,
Where every critter's wild and free.

In shadows deep, they dream and scheme,
Beneath the cones, they plot and beam.
A world of whimsy, always spun,
Where fitting in means having fun.

Conspiracies Within the Canopy

In the treetops high and bright,
Birds and squirrels plan at night.
With a wink, they plot their fun,
While the moonlight dances and runs.

Acorns fall like secret notes,
As owls in cloaks take to their coats.
A whisper here, a giggle there,
Postcards sent to the bear in despair!

The leaves rustle with playful schemes,
While branches bounce with giggly dreams.
A secret club of sprightly kin,
Where every entrance wears a grin.

So climb on high, if you can dare,
Join the antics of woodland flair.
In the canopy, conspiracies play,
Where laughter rules both night and day.

The Silent Guardian of the Glade

In the woods where whispers grow,
A squirrel claims the starry show.
He pats the ground with tiny paws,
While the owls giggle, "What a cause!"

A deer winks as it sips from streams,
Chasing shadows, caught in beams.
Its antlers shake with laughter loud,
As bunnies hide beneath a cloud.

The laughter echoes through the air,
While tree trunks boast of their fine hair.
"Who's the guardian?" they softly say,
"Just a chipmunk leading the fray!"

In this glade, all rules unwind,
Where every twist is well-defined.
The trees are wise, but what a fuss,
With secret jokes they share with us.

Veils of Enigma in the Pines

Among the pines, a riddle lies,
With dancing shadows in disguise.
A mischievous sprite pulls at the breeze,
Tickling trees with playful tease.

The wind whispers, "Catch me, please!"
While critters join the game with ease.
An owl says, "I know where to hide,"
As all the others burst with pride.

A rabbit hops and spills the beans,
Chortling softly behind the scenes.
"Tonight's the night for silliness,"
As raccoons wear hats to impress!

So here we sit, a merry bunch,
In nature's lap, we savagely munch.
With veils of fun, we bask and play,
In the pines where riddles sway.

Echoes of Forgotten Footprints

Footprints lead a merry trail,
A bunny follows, quick as a sail.
"Who left these marks?" it asks the air,
A songbird chirps, "A friend, I swear!"

The path is lined with giggles light,
As foxes play, igniting the night.
"Let's chase the shadows," they all agree,
"Who knows what laughs we'll set free!"

With every step, the echoes play,
In this woodland ballet of sway.
Trees chuckle low, branches sway,
"Just fooling around—come join our play!"

And when the moon begins to glow,
The forest revels, putting on a show.
In echoes soft, we find our place,
Where laughter lingers, a warm embrace.

Beneath the Boughs of Mystery

Beneath the boughs, a jester sings,
A hedgehog dons its finest things.
"Why so prickly?" the raccoon quips,
"Because I'm the life of all the trips!"

With giggles rolling like a stream,
The foxes gather, plotting a scheme.
"Let's prank the owl that snores at night,"
They snicker and waddle, full of delight.

Each bough holds cozy tales untold,
Of lively characters, brave and bold.
Beneath the canopy, laughter abounds,
In each hidden nook, a giggle resounds.

So come and join this merry quest,
With creatures wild who jest the best.
For in this realm of mystery,
There's humor wrapped in history.

Unspoken Promises of the Trees

Whispers tickle in the breeze,
Branches gossip while we tease.
Leaves chatter as they sway,
Promises made in a playful way.

A squirrel winks, a bird will giggle,
Underneath, the roots do wiggle.
Who knows what the moss might tell?
In this wood, all serves to quell.

Shade does laugh, light dapples down,
The trees wear humor like a crown.
Bark around us starts to grin,
A twist of joy where paths begin.

In the dusk, the shadows play,
Jokes exchanged in a cheeky sway.
Rustling leaves, a playful shout,
In this realm, fun's never out.

Rituals of the Woodland Whisper

In the woods where giggles rise,
Foliage twirls and none disguise.
With each rustle, laughter spills,
Whispers hold all the woodland thrills.

A chipmunk dons a tiny hat,
While beetles dance, imagine that!
Twigs tap-tap in a merry beat,
Nature's jive, can't be beat.

With a twig as a magic wand,
The fairies twirl on leafy pond.
Owl hoots jokes from high above,
In every nook, there's laughter's love.

At sunset's glance, they'd frolic bold,
The forest secrets yet untold.
In shadows thick, they share a jest,
At nightfall, nature's very best.

The Tapestry of the Timbered Grove

A tapestry woven green and gold,
With threads of humor brightly told.
Each branch a story, each leaf a laugh,
The timbered grove's no dainty staff.

Mossy carpets where critters prance,
Fungi join in the woodland dance.
Branches wave in a playful way,
Sharing tales of their funny day.

A squirrel jumps, a crow takes flight,
Lying low, the bushes ignite.
Crisp shells crack with echoing sound,
Each laugh festers in every round.

Dappled light plays merry tricks,
Nature's punchlines come in flicks.
In this grove, all are charmed,
With joy wrapped around, disarmed.

Intrigue Among the Bark and Branch

In the woods, where mysteries thrive,
The bark has tales where laughs derive.
Branches curtsy in shadows shy,
Sprightly secrets flutter and fly.

A woodpecker spies with a twinkling eye,
Amidst the drama, squirrels ask why.
With acorns stacked in a silly heap,
The forest keeps joy in its deep.

Whimsical whispers fill the air,
Rabbits chatter with zealous flair.
Every knot in the tree holds glee,
In this plot, merriment's key.

A shadow leaps, concocting plots,
As sunlight spills on mischief spots.
Among the bark, the chuckles blend,
An intriguing realm, where fun won't end.

Quiet Stories of the Timbered Realms

In the shade where branches twist,
A squirrel plots with a flick of his wrist.
Whispered tales of nuts not shared,
A dance of shadows, none prepared.

The owls chuckle as they sway,
Misplacing their glasses at the end of the day.
Mice gossip of the cheese mystery,
Each crumb a laugh, a tale's history.

The trees, they creak, with laughter loud,
While the wind joins in, feeling proud.
A standoff between the fox and the hare,
Who wins the race? It's all just flare!

The grasshoppers join in can-can cheer,
With leaps and hops, drawing near.
Under the trunk, a puppet show,
With acorns as tickets to the grand glow.

Secrets Wrapped in Brown and Green

Beneath the boughs the mischief brews,
A hedgehog giggles at the squirrel's shoes.
Thorns are ticklish, who knew that could be?
An elf's lost cap, what a sight to see!

With brambles acting like a spy,
They eavesdrop on gossip as birds fly by.
A lizard chuckles, well-played disguise,
As trees wink proudly, with leafy lies.

The mushrooms pretend they're the talk of the town,
While beetles parade, with swagger and frown.
They whisper of adventures beneath the moon,
Even the crickets are humming a tune.

But in this realm, where shadows play,
Every twig tells stories, in its own way.
A bear takes a nap, and dreams of a feast,
As nature's circus welcomes the least!

The Heartbeat of the Silent Woods

The heartbeat echoes, as trees begin to dance,
With roots all tangled in a funny romance.
Bees wear bowties and buzz about,
Throwing a party, with little doubt.

The mushrooms twirl in their polka dot hats,
While the rabbits hop and change many stats.
A dance-off ensues, it's truly a sight,
When shadows spin under the pale moonlight.

A fox tells jokes to a crowd of the brave,
While the owls hoot tales of the paths they pave.
The whispers in the breeze, a chuckling cheer,
A symphony of nature that all can hear.

Laughter leaks out from the cracks in the bark,
As the trees share secrets with a bark.
In this silent realm where joy holds the rod,
Life's just a riddle, but not one that's flawed!

The Enigma of Gnarled Limbs

With gnarled limbs, the trees pose a riddle,
While the raccoons play a merry little fiddle.
A twist of a branch, a chuckle bestowed,
As laughter echoes down the woodland road.

The squirrels act foolish, with flips in the air,
While the wise old tree just stands and stares.
A group of mosquitoes form a tiny band,
Their music's a buzz—a curious strand.

Frogs croak jokes while the beetles tap dance,
The whole forest laughs, caught in a trance.
Each knotted branch shares a story untold,
Of friendships and follies from ages of old.

In this realm of whimsy, where mischief is keen,
Every nook holds a laugh, a sight to be seen.
So join in the joy, let your spirits bloom,
For nature's a jester, in leaf and in loom!

The Forest's Mosaic of Whispers

In the woods where creatures laugh,
A squirrel holds a photograph.
With acorns dressed in grand array,
It tells the tales of yesterday.

The shadows dance with vibrant glee,
A raccoon plans a jubilee.
He juggles nuts while things grow wild,
The trees look on with laughter mild.

Old owls hoot their merry tune,
While rabbits hop beneath the moon.
The ferns all sway, a playful sight,
As crickets chirp throughout the night.

So wander in this playful glade,
Where mischief blooms and plans are laid.
For every rustle, every cheer,
A giggle hides, both near and dear.

The Allure of the Mischievous Mistletoe

Beneath the boughs where shadows play,
A sprightly kiss can lead astray.
With mistletoe, the prankster's charm,
Entices lovers, but causes harm.

The squirrels chuckle at the sight,
A portrait done in pure delight.
While cheeky birds eye their next snack,
They plot and scheme, then dive right back.

Oh, holiday spirit wrapped in fun,
A tangle made for everyone.
But lift your head, and you might find,
A cheeky grin, a jest entwined.

So swing beneath the kiss that's bold,
As laughter weaves through branches old.
Here, hearts will flutter, faces red,
While jests abound, and joy is spread.

Evergreen Elegies and Ancient Lore

Once whispered tales in trunks so grand,
Of love, mischief, and a band.
The pine trees sigh with every breeze,
As stories float like honeyed teas.

The beetles dance with flair and zest,
While woodpeckers drum, a lively fest.
Fungi giggle at the passing tales,
In leafy homes where laughter prevails.

With roots entwined in whispers deep,
A fortune told from dreams we keep.
Can you hear the laughter in the leaves?
A riddle shared, no one believes.

So tread lightly on this playful ground,
Where echoes of jest are always found.
In every branch, a chuckle rings,
The trees may speak of silly things.

The Constellations of Rooted Mystery

Stars twinkling through the forest veil,
Bears dance 'round, a merry tale.
With every step, a giggle hides,
In tangled vines where joy abides.

The night owl hoots, a beady eye,
As fireflies wink and float on by.
They map the night with sparkles bright,
Creating laughter in sheer delight.

The foxes plot beneath the skies,
With secret tricks in sly disguise.
While hedgehogs snicker, munching snails,
In private jokes and clever trails.

So wander through this cosmic dance,
Where mischief and the moon enhance.
In every shadow, giggles bloom,
As laughter lingers in the gloom.

Beneath the Layered Leaves

Beneath the green, a squirrel peeks,
With acorns hidden, his stash he keeps.
Whispers of crumbs and chuckles abound,
As critters gather with nibbles profound.

An owl hoots loud, claiming the night,
While raccoons dance in the soft moonlight.
In leafy homes, they tell tales so grand,
Of mischief and fun, all perfectly planned.

The wind carries laughter, echoes of play,
As branches sway in a light-hearted sway.
They giggle and chuckle, the forest's delight,
In this zany realm, everything's bright.

So under the boughs of an old, twisted tree,
Let's join in the jests, come share in the glee.
For laughter and fun in this space intertwine,
In a world where the whimsical always will shine.

Forest Whispers on the Wind

The trees share stories, all dressed in green,
Of chipmunk escapades that can't be unseen.
Socks and shoes, they can't seem to find,
While owls point fingers, laughing behind.

A rabbit jumps high, trying to brag,
But face-plants hard with a comical wag.
The fox rolls his eyes at the goofy display,
As forest's companions all join in the play.

Rustling leaves tune the laughter's sweet sound,
While mushrooms giggle from under the ground.
They plot pranks and puns, all in good cheer,
With nature as witness to each silly sneer.

So hear what they tell in the whispers of trees,
Embrace the peculiarity, let's do as we please.
A rollicking romp where the wild things reside,
In the company of joy, no need to hide.

Silent Legends of the Elders

Old trees stand tall, with wisdom to share,
Though they often mumble in rhymes full of flair.
"We've seen a few squirrels trip over their toes,
And bears who've mistaken a rock for a rose!"

Among gnarled roots, the stories unfold,
Of moles having feasts, in their burrows so bold.
In the soft mossy beds, they chuckle and scheme,
As the wind tickles leaves, igniting their dream.

With whispers of humor that linger, delight,
They recount how a crow stole a cake from a kite.
"Life's funny like that," the old trees would say,
"Just laugh at the chaos and dance through the fray!"

For legends may whisper, but laughter is loud,
In the heart of the woods, together we're proud.
A jaunt through the forest, let's frolic and grin,
In this realm of the odd where the fun shall begin.

The Unfolding of Nature's Mystique

With petals aglow and buds bursting wide,
Blossoms gossip while bees gently bide.
A turtle in slippers rolls right off the path,
While ladybugs giggle, sharing the laughs.

The creek bubbles softly, with ripples of cheer,
As frogs leap around, full of whimsy and beer.
They croak out nonsense under the moon's soft light,
Creating a chorus that dances through night.

The breeze carries whispers of legends untold,
Of critters in costumes, both daring and bold.
Fawns with their antics, a comedic parade,
In wild, merry antics, pure joy is displayed.

So drink from the laughter that nature bestows,
And join in the fun as the wild garden grows.
Together we'll twirl, in this riddle we weave,
Where the mirth of the forest, none can believe!

Enigmas Entwined Within the Wild

In the woods, a squirrel pranks,
Hiding nuts in curious banks.
He giggles as he climbs so high,
While trees above just laugh and sigh.

A rabbit thinks he's found a clue,
But it's just an old, forgotten shoe.
With whispers soft, the ferns conspire,
To keep their jokes just out of fire.

Beneath the boughs, a shadow peeks,
A raccoon plotting, oh what sneaks!
He hides a stash of shiny things,
In laughter, the forest softly sings.

The owls, wise in their delight,
Tell stories in the day and night.
They chuckle low, as pods break free,
In the whimsical, woodsy spree.

Labyrinths of Leaves and Light

In a twisty maze of sun-drenched green,
A butterfly flirts, all spry and keen.
With every flap, it twists and turns,
While flowers giggle, their colors churn.

A fox, with a grin, slides to the scene,
Sneaking peeks where he's never been.
With leaves that rustle a playful tune,
He's sure the sun is a giant balloon.

A stout old hedgehog waddles fast,
In search of riddles, a curious blast.
He ponders deeply by a prickly bush,
Where shadows play and giggles rush.

The forest hums with whispered cheer,
As creatures dance, from far and near.
In labyrinths of chirps and sights,
The silly woods hold pure delights.

The Forest Keeper's Untold Tales

The keeper chuckles, walking slow,
As tiny paws make quite the show.
With birds that gossip and chitchat loud,
He rolls his eyes, beneath the cloud.

A log that's a throne for ants so bold,
Holds stories of treasures, yet untold.
They march in lines, so proud and sure,
While the keeper shakes his head, demure.

A toadstool hosts a birthday bash,
With mushrooms dancing in a flash.
The keeper laughs at their wild spree,
As he sips tea from an acorn spree.

While shadows grow and sunsets glow,
His tales unwind, a breezy flow.
With laughter ringing through the night,
The woods ignite with pure delight!

The Veil of Verdant Dreams

In a cloak of green where giggles play,
Lies a patch of dreams that twist and sway.
A parrot mimics all the chatter,
While fairies laugh at silly matter.

Each leaf holds a tale, a jolly jest,
In whispers shared, they feel so blessed.
A chipmunk sings a silly song,
With jingling notes where he belongs.

The dappled sun casts a dancing glow,
Painted by breezes, where secrets flow.
Mushrooms peek from under the shade,
Their little hats too funny to be played.

With rustling laughs, the stream joins in,
Tickling stones with a giggling din.
The veil of dreams wraps round with cheer,
In this woodsy world, nothing's unclear!

Echoes of Ancients in the Bark

The trees are wise, or so they say,
Whispering tales from the good old days.
Squirrels jest, spinning yarns on the breeze,
While branches chuckle, giggling with ease.

Old knots hold laughter and hidden dreams,
A lost sock here or a nut that gleams.
Each bark's a canvas, each ring a laugh,
Nature's own stand-up, a quirky path.

Pine cones clack in a musical jibe,
As critters boast of their woodland tribe.
With a wink from a crow and a glance from a fox,
The forest's alive with its merry parox.

Secrets galore in a woodsy show,
Where the funny burble of life does flow.
So tiptoe lightly, and lend an ear,
For the trees might just share a joke or a cheer.

The Crystal Clear Hush of the Pines

In the hush of the pines, where giggles reside,
Fragrant whispers of folly do hide.
Stuffed critters pretending to nap in the sun,
Are plotting a party—oh, this will be fun!

Beneath the boughs, an acorn ballet,
Hosted by squirrels in a jolly display.
Each twirling flop full of carefree delight,
As the moon peeks through for a late-night sight.

Branches sway, and a raccoon gives chase,
Through a loopty-loo dance in a vibrant space.
With a twinkling giggle and limited flair,
The pines offer laughter—better than air!

So join the fun in this leafy retreat,
Where nature's quirks provide smiles so sweet.
Amidst the stillness, hear nature conspire,
Tales of the wood should never expire.

Shadows Dancing in the Understory

Under shadows where mischief may dwell,
Lies a playful scene; oh, can you tell?
Tiny frogs cheer with a ribbit and leap,
While worms argue who has the best sleep.

Mushrooms poke fun, with their hats all askew,
"Who needs a twig?" they say, "We've got a view!"
As rabbits race past in an amusing embrace,
Unruly antics keep time with the pace.

The ferns sway along with a whimsical beat,
While raccoons juggle their cans in the heat.
Nature's own circus, a hilarious spree,
Who knew the woods held such comedy?

So laugh away here in the vibrant hush,
With critters about, in a raucous rush.
Join in the dance, celebrate the sight,
For shadows bring smiles within the twilight.

The Palette of Nature's Secrets

Colors collide where the wild things roam,
Crafting a canvas that feels like home.
Sunshine giggles as it dapples the ground,
Painting the leaves in a riotous sound.

The reds whisper tales of mischief and cheer,
While yellows tease softly, "We're happy to be here!"
Oranges prance by with a festive pace,
Each hue a quirk in this woodland race.

Blues twirl merrily on a cool summer day,
Grinning while frolicking, come join our play!
Think green would be jealous, but it can't keep still,
It hums a sweet tune, beckoning the thrill.

Under this palette, nature's jesters unite,
Sharing their colors, a joyful delight.
So come, take a stroll where the fun never ends,
In a world where the colors are always best friends.

Guardians of the Gnarled Roots

In the woods where gnarled roots twist,
Squirrels plan a heist—who's on the list?
A stash of acorns, just for fun,
They giggle and scamper, on the run.

Mossy knights with hats so tall,
Arguing in whispers, 'Tis a grand ball!
A parade of gnomes with red-pointed caps,
Stumble over logs, they're caught in their naps.

Beneath the branches, tales abound,
Of trees that gossip without a sound.
Sticks eavesdrop on a bird who sings,
About the latest in squirrel flings!

With jests and jigs under the moon,
All the woodland critters swoon.
Watch closely now, as giggles rise,
For the roots hear it all, what a surprise!

The Soft Footfall of Secrets

Whispers travel through the cool night air,
Tiny feet tiptoe without a care.
A raccoon in a mask, oh so sly,
Checks his pockets, why oh why?

The pinecones giggle, rolling around,
While owls chuckle, perched on the ground.
A sassy fox with a twinkle in her eye,
Tries to convince a deer to fly!

Hidden treasures beneath the green,
A joke-telling badger, quite a scene.
Each clumsy paw makes laughter swell,
As critters share tales no one can tell.

Mischief brews in the shadowed glades,
Filled with whispers and escapades.
With every rustle, the fun begins,
In the ballet of woodland sins!

Beneath the Needle-Laden Horizon

Under needles where sunshine peeks,
Chipmunks hold conferences, oh what cheek!
With twigs for pens and leaves for notes,
They plan their pranks on all that floats.

A crow in a top hat recites a joke,
As squirrels laugh till they nearly choke.
Beetles tap dance on a twiggy floor,
While ladybugs watch and ask for more.

Among the shadows, a raccoon jests,
Bouncing around in his old-fashioned vests.
Mice in tuxedos, feeling so grand,
Line up for cheese—oh isn't it planned!

Oh, the tales of whimsy and delight,
In the evergreen air, it's quite the sight.
For each branch hides a playful ruse,
In this lively world where pranks amuse!

Shrouded in Pine: The Silent Saga

Tales weave through branches, light and spry,
With acorns conspiring as clouds float by.
A chipmunk's chuckle rings through the pine,
As rabbits join in, "Now that's divine!"

The wise old owl won't pick a side,
He just hoots along with amusing pride.
Squirrels debate who is the best,
In this raucous game of nutty jest.

Underneath the boughs, secrets replay,
Each skittering sound brings laughter at play.
What mischief awaits in the twilight mist?
A race for the nuts, oh can't be missed!

Now every creature knows the fun,
In a world where the giggles are never done.
With each new moon, they gather around,
For stories that echo and jokes profound!

Secrets of the Tall Green Guardians

In the forest so vast and grand,
The trees gossip, oh isn't it bland?
They whisper of squirrels, all hushed and shy,
Plotting their acorn heists on the sly.

With every rustle, a tale to be told,
Of raccoons and chipmunks, both foolish and bold.
A wedged pine's wisdom, a comical jest,
As the wind has a laugh with the birds as its guest.

A wise old tree with a trunk so wide,
Claims he once danced with the moon at high tide.
Yet every night when the stars shine bright,
He trips over roots in the pale moonlight.

So listen keenly as you tread near,
These tall green guardians are full of cheer.
They'll fill your heart with laughter and glee,
In their leafy realms, oh, what fun it can be!

Chambers of the Hidden Realm

Deep in the woods, a door made of bark,
Leads to a realm where the critters embark.
A hedgehog in slippers does tango with glee,
While fireflies flicker, lighting up the spree.

The mushrooms have tea parties, so quirky and spry,
Where whispers of wishes float up to the sky.
The gnomes all debate who will win in a race,
While the owls just hoot, they don't keep pace.

Rabbits in jackets discuss fashion trends,
As raccoons in bow ties play tricks on their friends.
But beware of the fox with the charming smile,
He'll steal your snacks and dance all the while!

The trees hold their laughter, their branches all sway,
In this secretive place, where the wild things play.
So venture inside, be ready for fun,
In the chambers where stories and giggles are spun!

Ghosts in the Green Embrace

Amidst the boughs, a spirit does sway,
With jokes so corny, they'll brighten your day.
He tickles the leaves as he drifts by the ground,
And his ghostly chuckles echo all around.

"You think you're scared?" he quips with a grin,
"I once lost my shoe in the woodpecker din!"
He floats to the brook for a sip of sweet dew,
Where the frogs croon soft tunes to the mild morning blue.

With twinkling eyes, he shares silly tales,
Of dancing with shadows and broomstick raids.
A chorus of laughter, the trees start to sway,
As the ghost shows the critters how to play.

So when the moon rises and silence takes hold,
Remember the ghost boy, both funny and bold.
He'll haunt your heart with joy and delight,
In the green embrace, making fears take flight!

The Untold Stories of Old Growth

Beneath the canopy, the giants stand tall,
Guardians of laughter, they cherish it all.
A squirrel spins tales of his daring crusade,
While the woodpecker rolls eyes at the escapade.

The elder tree chuckles, "You think that's a jest?
I once had a run-in with a hornet's nest!"
While fungi conspire to plot out a game,
With fairy lights twinkling adding to the fame.

A raccoon in goggles assembles a crew,
To raid the picnic—what's old is made new.
With stories of mishaps and each funny blunder,
These towering treasures keep secrets like thunder.

So wander on in, where the old tales reside,
Amongst the ancients where whimsy won't hide.
For in every rustle and tickle of the breeze,
Lies the laughter and joy of the grand evergreen trees!

Whispers in the Woven Boughs

In twisted trunks, the squirrels conspire,
Nuts and tales, they secretly acquire.
With giggles masked in rustling leaves,
They plot and scheme as the woodpecker thieves.

A raccoon winks at the owl up high,
"I'll steal your dinner, just you try!"
Beneath the canopy where mischief reigns,
Laughter spins through the leafy lanes.

The mossy floor, a stage for jest,
Where hedgehogs waddle, they love their fest.
A party brewed in the underbrush,
With brambles and blooms, oh what a hush!

In every knot, a tale resides,
As chatter bounces from boughs to sides.
High above, a breeze brings cheer,
In this merry place, we shed our fear.

Shadows Beneath the Needles

Beneath the arms of evergreens,
The chatter flows like bubbling streams.
Shadowy figures dance and sway,
In quirky games, they spend the day.

A chipmunk dons a tiny hat,
Proclaiming he's the king, just look at that!
With a wink and hop, he leads the way,
As critters follow, in bright array.

The badgers play cards, their faces grim,
While the fox plays tricks with an acorn whim.
Each snicker adds to the forest tune,
As laughter echoes 'neath the silver moon.

With every rustle, a joke unspooled,
In nature's theater, we all are schooled.
The joy of whispers, so rich and deep,
In shadows where the woodland creatures leap.

The Hidden Echoes of the Forest

Echoes flutter, a merry blend,
From branches swaying, around they bend.
A chorus sneaks through the tangled green,
Of giggling sprites, a playful scene.

A hedgehog tells tales of heroic fights,
With butterflies playing the best of sights.
They clap their wings in delightful cheer,
As the sun dips low, their songs we hear.

Woodpeckers drum in a comedic clash,
While raccoons roll 'neath a fallen ash.
The forest floor, a stage so bright,
Where laughter flows till the fall of night.

Secrets linger in each soft swoosh,
Of playful pranks that make them woosh.
In this wild world, both odd and grand,
Lies joy where friendship takes a stand.

Veils of Verdant Mystery

In veils of green, the antics thrive,
Where every critter feels alive.
A possum swings from a lowly branch,
Claiming it's all just a silly dance.

The porcupine grins with quills so sharp,
As rabbits play tunes on an acorn harp.
Balancing acts of utmost glee,
With giggles shared in a bushy spree.

Mossy thrones hold the laughing crowd,
Their playful shouts rise up so loud.
In tangled roots, their secrets stay,
A whimsical world where we all play.

Beneath the boughs, a party awaits,
With stories spun by mischievous fates.
So join the fray in this leafy nook,
Escape the gloom and take a look!

Conspiracies Among the Canopy

Squirrels gather, plotting all day,
Whispering tales while hiding their prey.
Mossy hats and nutty schemes,
Beneath the branches, they chase their dreams.

Robins giggle at the tales they spin,
Of who stole what, and where they've been.
The acorns roll as laughter flies,
In the treetops, truth wears a disguise.

Badgers and foxes, feigning their snooze,
Gossiping close, sharing the news.
Every rustle, a raucous delight,
In the leafy world, mysteries take flight.

Tales from the Silent Grove

In the shade where shadows play,
The owls nod off at end of day.
Raccoons trade snacks with giggles and grins,
Tonight's the night for their game of sins.

A deer sidles up with a tale to tell,
Of how the porcupine once miscast a spell.
"Over there," she points with a flourish and flair,
"Is a rabbit who's convinced it can fly in the air!"

Whispers float on the sweet night breeze,
Of creatures conspiring with utmost ease.
They lift each other's spirits so grand,
In this timbered realm where friendships expand.

Enigmas Wrapped in Evergreen

In green cloaks, the trees share a wink,
As the winds carry tales of the creatures who think.
A chipmunk once thought it could drive a car,
The whole forest laughed, his fame spread afar.

Foxes with maps, counting their tricks,
Plotting to learn all the best little clicks.
They sneak through the shadows, their tails held high,
While the ponderous owl just rolls his eye.

The ferns rustle softly, they join in the jest,
As raccoons bond over twinkling fest.
In the depth of the grove, with giggles that soar,
Who knew the woods held so much to explore?

Fragments of the Forgotten Wood

In the depths where the ferns intertwine,
A gnome croaks jokes with a goblet of wine.
He says, "Did you hear about the hare's new hat?
He wears it so proud, it's the talk of the mat!"

The mushrooms are chuckling, they can't get enough,
While the hedgehogs debate if the snacks are too tough.
A pixie twirls 'round like a whirling kite,
With whispers of mischief dancing in flight.

Crickets play tunes for the moon to embrace,
While fireflies flicker in a merry race.
With gossip and laughter, the night glows bright,
In this wood of whimsy, life's sheer delight.

www.ingramcontent.com/pod-product-compliance
Lightning Source LLC
Chambersburg PA
CBHW071844160426
43209CB00003B/410